The Muse as I Hear Her

The Muse as I Hear Her

Giles Pickford

Published by ANU eView
The Australian National University
Canberra ACT 0200, Australia
Email: anuepress@anu.edu.au
This title is also available online at http://eview.anu.edu.au

---

National Library of Australia Cataloguing-in-Publication entry

Author: Pickford, Giles, author.

Title: The muse as I hear her / Giles Pickford.

ISBN: 9781921934131 (paperback) 9781921934148 (ebook)

Subjects: Australian poetry.

Dewey Number: A821.4

All rights reserved. No part of this publication may be reproduced, stored in a retrieval system or transmitted in any form or by any means, electronic, mechanical, photocopying or otherwise, without the prior permission of the publisher.

All photos from Giles Pickford's private collection except where otherwise indicated

© Giles Pickford 2013

This edition © 2013 ANU eView

Contents

Foreword to *The Muse as I Hear Her* ix
   James J. Fox

The Soul 1
Haiku for Eve and Pandora 2
Faith Hope and Love 4
Cain 5
The Snake Replies 6
A Handful of Symbols 7
17 Questions without Answers 8
The Ballad of Old Kirrawee 9
A Nonsense Rhyme for a Senseless Time 10
On the 3rd Anniversary of the New ACT House of Assembly:
A cartoon in verse 11
On the Unlikely Possibility that there are First and Last in People 13
Seven, Eleven, Nine 14
Paroo, Bokhara, Warrego, Irrara 15
Just as Well 17
Ode to Christchurch 18
Haiku for Taiwan 19
Diplomatic Incident: Coombs Car Park 20
Leviathan, Ziz and Behemoth 21
Sedition is Curved 22
Random Patterns on a Screen 23
On the Unlikely Possibility that there are First Causes
   in the Universe 24
Things you will never ever know 25
Numbers after Heisenberg, 1927 26
A Haiku on People who are Always Complaining 27
The Angle of Repose 28
Déjà Prévu (Already Foreseen) 29
On Our Ruby Wedding Day 30
About the author 31

Dedicated to Polyhymnia: the Muse of Sacred Poetry

Foreword to *The Muse as I Hear Her*

This volume, *The Muse as I Hear Her*, has been compiled at the urging of ANU Emeritus Faculty. It is intended to honour Giles Pickford, an admired colleague of long standing. Giles was employed at the ANU for ten years. He officially began his appointment in the ANU Public Affairs Division on the 21st of November 1988 and he retired on the 8th of May 1998. At that time, a group of colleagues had formed an association that was to become the ANU Emeritus Faculty. From 1998 to the end of 2012, Giles was Secretary to the Emeritus Faculty. He served the Emeritus Faculty for a longer period than he was officially employed at ANU. Until recently he continued in the role of Corresponding Secretary, but health intervened at the age of 73. He can no longer drive because of vertigo and so his visits to Canberra have been curtailed.

As members of the Emeritus Faculty, we wanted to honour Giles for his good fellowship and for the many services he rendered to the Faculty. After various discussions, we decided to highlight one of Giles' special interests – his close involvement in the ANU Poets' Lunch.

The Poets' Lunch is an ANU institution that has gone through various incarnations. Begun informally in the 1970s by ANU-based poets such as A. D. Hope, R. F. Brissenden, Geoff Page, Rosemary Dobson and others, this first generation would meet on occasion at the ANU Staff Centre. At these lunches they fashioned poems in praise of wine.

In time this founding generation ceased to gather. In consequence, in 1993, at a celebration in the Great Hall of University House held to honour A. D. Hope, Giles and Colin Plowman were charged with reviving the traditions of the ANU Poets' Lunch. They succeeded and a second generation of lunches began. The scope of these lunches was expanded and Giles became a key participant in this next generation until his retirement in 1998.

Subsequently, a third generation has taken up the traditions of the ANU Poets' Lunch. Gatherings are now held at the Emeritus Faculty. Members of this third generation suggested this volume of Giles' poetry be put together as an appropriate tribute from the ANU Emeritus Faculty. David Walker prepared the compilation and with Giles' assistance, he collected some of the photographs in the volume. Others have come from the ANU Archives.

This volume is thus a token of recognition from friends and colleagues to Giles Pickford – for his multiple contributions to the life of the University and its community.

James J. Fox

Chair, ANU Emeritus Faculty

Giles and Jan Eagleton display some of the promotional material for the ANU sesquicentenary 1996

Photo courtesty ANU Archives

The Soul

A baby sparrow fell from its nest. I was 6.
We took it in and fed it with an eyedropper.
We called it Cherub.

It snuggled into my cupped hand
Sleeping with its chin on my thumb

I am now 71 and remember Cherub
It resembles a soul in my mind.
It has no weight, it is hungry and it is helpless.

Thousands don't believe it exists.

But I have held it in my hand and cherished it.

It exists across the entire universe.
It has no weight, it is everywhere and nowhere.
It is hungry and helpless.

Thousands are wrong. It exists.

May 1947 and May 2011

Haiku for Eve and Pandora

According to the Torah, the Bible, and the Qur'an, Eve was the first woman created by Yahweh, God, and Allah. According to the Greek Myths, Pandora was the first woman on earth. Both women were set up to take the blame for everything that has ever gone wrong: an idea which is rebarbative in the present age. My mother was born in 1907 and was one of the first feminists. She gave me a point of view which is expressed here.

Eve in the Garden
First woman, primordial one
She the innocent

Pandora with three boxes

Pandora, doomed one
Intellectual enquiry
Curiosity

Pandora and Eve
Spirit of discovery
Both wanting to know

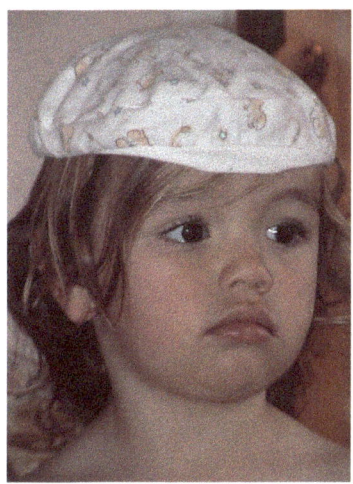

Defiant Eve

Eve and Pandora
Both born in the human spring
Scapegoats framed for us

Both take all the blame
The evil that from them came
Allocated shame

Sad Pandora or Eve

****

My wife rails at me
"It's your fault all this went wrong!"
Eve takes her just revenge

Pictures printed with the permission of the Author's granddaughter, Madeline Gass, who is now a charming young woman of nine and likely to take after her great grandmother from what I have seen so far.

Published in the 2009 ANU Poets' Lunch (theme: Pandora's Box)

Faith Hope and Love

There are faith hope and love
Love is the greatest of these.
There are love hope and faith
In faith we face the unknown.
There are hope faith and love
Without all three we're alone.

But hope must be the stone
On which the foundations rest.
Bereft of hope, love and faith
Are birds without a nest.

Cain

Born in the first unwanted pregnancy
After the eviction from paradise
Cain arrives with a rock in his hand
To smash the skull of the favoured child
And become the first murderer in the land

The Snake Replies

Snakes always speak in blank verse. Rhyming is too far off the ground and it makes them giddy.

	O
Me? Cold-blooded? Nonsense!	III
	III
I am the temperature of my ambience.	III
	III
I lie on a hot rock and I am 40 degrees.	III
	III
The temperature drops and I sleep.	III
	III
You would die on the rock and freeze at night.	III
	III
I have no limbs.	III
	III
And so have no circulatory disorders.	III
	II
I only need to eat twice a week.	III
	III
I have only one enemy: you.	III
	III
You are surrounded by enemies.	III
	II
I would never swap places with you.	I
	!

To be published in the 2013 Poets' Lunch at ANU (theme: Cold-blooded things)

A Handful of Symbols

The first finger points and accuses
Second is longest: its gesture is obscene
The third bears the ring of faithfulness
The fourth is prayerful and serene

Strong thumb is one and all alone
And for ever will oppose them

17 Questions without Answers

Who allows those two addicts to have
that bright-eyed unwanted child? Who permits
the child's teacher to abuse a position
of trust? Did both create the arsonist?
And was his hangman duly licensed?

Who licences Scrooge to grind the faces of
the poor? By what right does the Warder
curtail the liberty of the oppressed?
Who authorises the purblind torturer?
What principle permits the just war?

By what authority does the polyp
make a reef? What guides the rambling vine?
What force informs unravelling history?
What anvil forges the incandescent Tiger?
Is blind nature licensed or unlicensed?

Who licences Poets, who are "the mirrors
of the gigantic shadows which futurity
casts upon the present"? Was it Shelley?
Who licences the giver of licences?

All poets are licensed; but, are some
more licentiously licensed than others?

Published in the 2008 ANU Poets' Lunch (theme: Poetic Licence)

The Ballad of Old Kirrawee

This is the Ballad of brave Faherty
Who loved a fair maiden in Old Kirrawee
Up on the moors he bended his knee
And offered his troth beneath a green tree

Maeve was her name, her hair was jet black
It fell in soft waves all down her sweet back
Her eyes were deep blue, and she had a knack
Of driving men wild by selling them Smack

A hooker was she, a pusher as well
Poor brave Faherty was going to Hell
When for this wild maiden he stupidly fell
No matter what happened their love didn't jell

Up on the wild moors of Old Kirrawee
He tied a strong rope to the same green tree
Where he'd declared his love on bended knee
Thus ended the life of poor Faherty

Those who pass by the moor are taken aback
By the Ghosts of both lovers up on the track
He with the rope hanging from his poor neck
And she with the blue eyes selling him Smack

Assisted by Bruichladdich Islay Malt

Boxing Day 2007

A Nonsense Rhyme for a Senseless Time

The people of Catamite thought
That the Minister ought to do nought
For grinding the cattle
And pounding the pratal
Were all that the good people sought

The Tsunaminous Minister fought
To change all the rules which he thought
Were 'holding us back
And creating a crack
In the Cateconomic Report'

All vassals were turned into clowns
All verbs were changed into nouns
All customs were cancelled
All missions enhancelled
All caps were strategically crowns

The Minister got what he wanted
The fonts were slowly disconted
The cattle ungrounded
The pratal impounded
The Catamites sad and garronted

Although the Catamites mourned
The Minister's face was adorned
On History's fair page
For age after age
While his subject's belongings were pawned

Published in the 2005 ANU Poets' Lunch

On the 3rd Anniversary of the New ACT House of Assembly: A cartoon in verse

The Sun came up rosy on that frabjous day
When the people's champions gathered for the fray,
Beneath Ethos' statue they sat fumbling,
The proud and humble together mumbling,
Waiting for Roberta's call to order,
Awed, nervous and awkward, dressed nattily,
Aware of strife within the border
Of Australia's newest Principality.

McRae gave the signal, up they rose,
Ritualistically rising on their toes,
Whilst the gloomy citizenry,
With knotted brows and clasped hands,
Wondered if all would be good and well
This thought occurred also to Kate Carnell.

Wayne Berry, battle hard and jolly,
Victor of the skirmish known as the Visiting Medical Officers Folly
Was flanked by his Chief, Rosemary Follett,
Champion of the Legislature,
Gentle in look, merciless in nature.
Then came Bill Wood and Terry Conolly,
Governing town and school lawfully,
Solemn and riven by the awful plight
Of representing the Centre and the Right.
Ellis, Elinor and Lamont then emerge,
Walking backwards to protect the rear

Of fledgling Government from the scourge
Of Stevenson rumbling in hot pursuit;
And Humphries, sad-eyed and hirsute.
Then De Domenico, righter than right,
Kaine and Westende, walking slowly through the arch
Preserving their dignity. Ah! might is trite
At the tail-end of a triumphal march.

Last to join the panoplied processors
Were Szuty and Moore, the town's confessors,
Veterans of the lust industry debate,
Deciders of the dying person's fate,
One barbigerous the other not,
Ending the processional sentence with
The necessary dot.

Arriving a little late, Greg Cornwell,
Deputy Speaker, a man well used
To being terminally confused,
Noticed a vast wraith athwart the theatre.
He recognised in its jovial features
Hector Kinloch, forty feet in stature,
Smiling down upon his fellow creatures
As they entered the newest Legislature.

Published in ANU Poets' Lunch 1996

On the Unlikely Possibility that there are First and Last in People

Some people see themselves as first and some as last. But there is no difference. Money distorts their perceptions, acting like a curved mirror.

First will be last
And last will be first
An atom divides
A drink from a thirst

What is the difference
Between tycoon and bum?
One takes Gin, the other Rum
One a loaf, the other, crumb

The rich and the poor
Are joined at the hip
There's interdependence
In the rise and the dip

Wealthy and prisoner
Suffer rigidity
Both have to live in
Gated aridity

Published in the ANU Poets' Lunch, 2007 (Theme: First and Last Things)

Seven, Eleven, Nine

We eat and drink each day, for
Hunger obscures the pointless
Repetition of it all.

But there is a thirst from which
The untouched moment arrives.
Unknowable except by

A general assent amongst
The munchers and slurpers
That suddenly they are in

Unexplored Territory
The fog of sameness lifts and
We inhabit a new place.

The voices change and the faces are suffused
With the same light that saw Burke gazing on the Gulf,
Or the wonder of Giles at the western end
Of strata of colour beneath the blue.

This place can also be found solo.
But only out-of-doors when in the
Company of the many eyes that
Watch us when we eat beside the fire:
On the edge of a wild place, alone.

Published in the programme for the 1993 ANU Poets' Lunch. The obscurity of the title lifts when the number of syllables to the line is counted.

Paroo, Bokhara, Warrego, Irrara

Green flash of parrots through the gidgee,
Red glare of sun off the claypan floor,
Cold stars shine, night sounds quiver,
fire in the grate at the homestead door.

Dusty-breasted and perilous her loves
On the long rubble of the Yantabulla Road.

Lousy Jacks whoop on the Yellow Box twig
While red fox slinks below.
Wild boar roots near twenty-mile drain
Out back in the Brigalow.

Loving and dangerous she combs her hair
On the long dust of the Yantabulla Road.

Smoke in the eye, dew on the nose,
The sun rises slow on the edge of the world.
Ring around the Moon, rain on the gilgai,
These are the gifts of her love unfurled.

Patient, all-knowing, lonely she waits
On the long mud of the Yantabulla Road.

Bleached skull winks and willy willy laughs
In the barbed wire heat of the furnace days.
Iron lunged wind from the Bulloo overflow
Dries blood spit and tears in the noon day haze.

Lose her, and she will never find you
On the long dust of the Yantabulla Road.

Paroo, Bokhara, Warrego, Irrara,
On the long straight curve of the Yantabulla Road.

Bush Glossary

Gidgee: A type of mulga in the family Acacia

Lousy Jack: A pied Currawong prevalent on the North West Plains of NSW: Family - Artamidae; Order- Passeriformes

Gilgai: An area of flat ground that is under water when it rains. Try to drive across it then and you will sink to the axles. Walk across and you will sink to the ankles

Willy Willy: A tiny tornado only a foot across which can take your hat off and suck the tea out of your cup if it comes across you in the heat of the day.

Winner of the Traditional Bush Verse section 1990 Binalong Banjo Paterson Poetry Prize

Just as Well

It's just as well the sea
Will not rise over me,
Though myriads will flee
Poor Bangladesh and Zyder Zee.

It's just as well the drought
Will not see the winter out
At our resort strewn coast.
But burn wheat farms to toast.

It's just as well pestilence
Will meet with much resistance
From our well fed immunity,
But smite the poor community.

It's just as well the quake
Will not shake us all awake.
Though mothers' hearts may ache
In Bam and Sharm al Sheikh.

It's surely just as well.
But is it just, as well?

Published in the 2004 ANU Poets' Lunch

Ode to Christchurch

Christchurch people for day after day
Have suffered shock and grief so bitter
For months they've been shaken like the prey
In the jaws of a grim predator

The Earth heaved and seethed like boiling water
It melted like butter in the sun
There was little unbroken in Bexley
Bromley or Sumner once the quake was done

Their lives can never be the same again
Uncertainty lies beneath the ground
The bonds between women, children and men
Are all that's left which are strong and sound

But like light from a far off beacon
The distant sweetness of hope is found
Christchurch was and will be again
New Zealand's most beautiful town

with Tom Gregg

Haiku for Taiwan

1. For Mandy Lin
Taiwan dreams like an opal
Hidden in the China Sea
Beautiful is she.

2. For Professor Pierre Yang
Guns across the Strait we hear
Thunder from the Silent Zone
But can they hear us?

3. For Carlo Chen
Quietly they gather the
Two-leaf tea in Alishan
In a golden bowl

4. For Madame Pao-Chuan Chang
Danshui on the river mouth
History is in your bones
Children take your gift

5. For Stephen Liu
Teeming Taipei bursts with noise
But in the Martyrs' Shrine is
Silence of lost lives

6. For Lian-Cherng Tang
In Towradgi you found me
By the great blue southern sea
My eyes have opened

December 2005, after the Ceremony at the Fort San Domingo Museum, Taiwan

Diplomatic Incident: Coombs Car Park

Out back of the Coombs after a Public Lecture
Where Paul Dibb spoke with some conjecture
Of Australia's future defence posture
(Mate, no need to think what it'll cost yer!)

Some Diplomats from the recalcitrant north,
(Near north that is, not north of the fourth
parallel) were convulsed in a clatter of mirth
About the wide open coast of our part of Earth.

Staggering past in the afternoon's last gleam
Your unworthy servant caught on to their theme.
He interjected (forgetting about trade)
With this quarrelsome, undiplomatic tirade.

"Eminences, we Aussies are lacking in fear.
Think, when estimating your likely losses;
Australians would prefer to fight for a year
Than work one day for the bosses."

Leviathan, Ziz and Behemoth

The waxing waning wayward moon looks back from the horizon
Her shining path sprinkles across the vast gulf of water.
Two eyes are shining like arc welders. See, it is Leviathan
Glaring back from the edge of the globe intent on slaughter

His bowels house his motive force fed by the yellow rock whose
Hideous strength knows no containment. High on his shining back
He carries the many manifestations of Ziz: awaiting their cues
A buzzing fury of wasps and hornets impatient to attack

On the distant shore the massed herds of Behemoth graze and sleep
A dispersed force of a trillion parts driven by one mind
Whose piercing eye is aware of what approaches from the deep
Whose spies watch every street, whose hidden hands touch every kind.

We sacrificed to them; we gave them our gold and our young ones
We poor weak creatures who scurried around their legs fed this fear
The feverish nightmare has persisted down through all the aeons
Existing now in the massed military demigods of land, sea and air

The writer acknowledges the author of The Book of Job 41:1-34 for the inspiration.

Published in the ANU Poets' Lunch, 2010 (theme: Yetis, Yowies and Unicorns)

Sedition is Curved

The universe is curved and so is endless time.
The Earth's road is curved and all creatures walk this way.
There is something in it which hates a dead straight line.
So nature's lovely, curly, random shapes hold sway.

But there is one deadly straight unnatural force
Which shows its hatred for the universal curve.
Tyranny drives with great speed in linear course,
Piercing the rib cage of freedom. It does not swerve.

Sedition bows humbly to unnatural power.
Appearing bent, recalcitrant, with curled lip; it would
Resist tyranny at every turn, hour by hour
Until the universal arc of all that's good

Bends arrow, spear, sword, cannon, each linear thing
Into a rounder shape. Thus the great circle of time
Completes its perennial quest, eradicating
Cruellest tyranny, the most unnatural crime.

Published in the ANU Poets' Lunch, 2006 (Theme: Sedition)

Random Patterns on a Screen

My darkened computer screen looks back at me, empty.
Droplets from past sneezes are dotted across the dark.
The random pattern they make does tempt me
To see the arrangement of galaxies and stars.

Looking at the random pattern I hit upon a wheeze.
Is the scatter of the far-flung stars
The result of a colossal cosmic sneeze?

On the Unlikely Possibility that there are First Causes in the Universe

If something has no end, then can one suppose that it has no beginning?

If there is no beginning
Then ending is done
A circle is endless
Beginning is none

Eternal desire precedes
Cause and effect
It yearns for our love
Which we dare not reject

We are its reflection
It is our perfection
It reaches far back
Before the first night

Before the first light
Before the first sin
A world without end
Has no origin

The second of a pair of poems submitted to the Poets' Lunch at ANU in 2007, on the theme First and Last Things

Things you will never ever know

Inspired by Heisenberg's Principle of Uncertainty

The moment you are born and first see your mother
The moment when you die and last see your lover
The moment when sleep shuts the curtains of your mind
These are the moments you will never ever find

Nor will you ever know the nature of time
Nor the depth of space, nor the number nine
The Quark and the Lepton will not be understood
Nor will you comprehend the nature of The Good

Some people know that they are always right
That certainty is real does not cause them fright
But some are relaxed to know it is also true
The sum of one and one is approximately two

Numbers after Heisenberg, 1927

A number is an unsteady measure
Heisenberg told us so
Because nothing is still for a second
A snapshot is too slow

Some things move at tectonic speed
Some move faster than light
Accuracy is impossible
When a blur is in your sight

Australia moves north each year
At the rate that toe nails grow
But you set the whole room in a spin
With positional vertigo

That a number can be exact
Is a useful abstraction, but
Multiplication and division
Addition and subtraction
Momentum and position
Are rocks in liquefaction

Published in ANU Poets' Lunch, 2012 (theme: Playing with Numbers)

A Haiku on People who are Always Complaining

Man standing still accuses,
But running man excuses.
Man needs momentum.

The Angle of Repose

A talus slope achieves the angle of repose
The younger the slope the steeper
The older slope has a much milder incline
Its mildness betrays that it's deeper

It takes a long time to reduce the incline
Memories go back much longer
Not on the move, the rocks rest in their groove
Immobile, they know they are stronger

Young rivers fly like arrows down their slopes
Impatient to rush through the scattered moraine
Old rivers, unhurried, find what they seek
Meandering carefully all over the plain

To live forever is to know more, not less
To arrive there we must be motionless

Déjà Prévu (Already Foreseen)

Derelict age with mottled scaly skin
With fading rheumy eyes, limping and thin
Unsteady of stance with balance denied
An open mouth with dribble at the side
Colourless thinning out of falling hair
The day-long occupancy of the chair
Aching joint, gnarled knuckle and tired bone
The vacant stare of one all ways alone
Listless, joyless, poverty-stricken age
With random outbursts of impotent rage
Breathless, toothless, pointless, quiet despair
Prosthetic, pathetic, going nowhere
The musty rancid smell and rattling breath
Marks the long lonely intercept with death

The shimmering view from the mountain peak,
The immensity of past time loved and lost,
Such abundance of memory must speak
From its great fullness. Love won at such cost,
The brawling careless days of long ago,
The sappy happy rambling days of old,
The rise of love and children that follow;
Then that fever called work: which the honest hold
Hard, but is held easy by the hollow.
At last when the harvest is in and done
Debts are paid, children grown, working no more
He moves quietly by the sea in the sun.
He hears the curved waves drumming down the shore
And treasures the beauty while his time is run

Published in ANU Poets' Lunch 2011 (theme: Deja Vu)

On Our Ruby Wedding Day

Thank you, dear, for forty years,
For all our joy and all our tears,
For all our children, and all of theirs,
For taking pains and smoothing cares

For forty years I held your head
Against my heart and quietly said
'I love you'. And now I say
'With this Ruby I thee re-wed.
On our 40th Wedding Day.'

About the author

Giles Pickford BA (Hons) was born in Bombay in 1941. However, he spent most of his early years growing up on a farm near Albany, WA. He was educated at Albany High School and the University of Western Australia where he obtained a BA first class Honours degree majoring in English Literature.

After graduation he spent some time in a droving team near Shark Bay, WA, before succumbing to a career as a university administrator, specialising in the fields of event organisation, fund raising and public relations in general.

He has worked at the University of WA, UNE, AVCC, James Cook University, the Australian Cancer Society, the University of Wollongong and The Australian National University.

He served as an Alderman of the Wollongong City Council from 1985-88 and he has served two terms with the ACT Cultural Council from 1991-96. He recently retired as the Secretary of the ANU Emeritus Faculty, and Convenor of the ATEM Ghosts: both of them are organisations for retired people.

He worked until the age of 71, much of it in later years as a volunteer.

He wrote poems, mostly in later life, which he published on his own web site. He has been an active member of the various incarnations of the ANU Poets' Lunch: http://www.anu.edu.au/emeritus/poets/

This publication of his poems was undertaken by the Poets' Lunch at ANU assisted by the ANU Emeritus Faculty.